Lost Transmissions

Lost Transmissions

Poems

DAVID MEMMOTT

SERVING HOUSE BOOKS

2012

Lost Transmissions: Poetry and Prose

ISBN: 978-0-9858495-1-1

Cover image: David Memmott
Cover design: Kristin Summers & David Memmott
Author photo: Sue Memmott

"Where the Yellow Brick Road Turns West, was first published as a Poets & Writers/World Voices e-chapbook with an introduction by George Venn on Web del Sol website at: http://chapbooks.webdelsol.com/. "Legacy for Beachcombers," "Let 'Er Buck," and "If Orpheus Had Played the Sax," were published in Summer 2012 issue of *Elohi Gadugi Journal*. Several of these poems appeared in the self-published collection, *Giving It Away* (2009, Wordcraft of Oregon, LLC).

I would like to give grateful acknowledgement to the Playa Institute of Summer Lake, Oregon, where most of these poems were either completed or conceived during a four-week residency in March/April, 2012. More information at: www.playasummerlake.org.

Special thanks to my grandsons, Larry and Chance, for their inspiration, and to Walter Cummins, Thomas E. Kennedy, Duff Brenna, George Venn, and David Axelrod for suggestions and, most of all, to my wife, Sue, for her love and support.

Serving House Books logo by Barry Lereng Wilmont
Published by Serving House Books
Copenhagen, Denmark and Florham Park, NJ

www.servinghousebooks.com

First Serving House Books Edition 2012

For all those whose lives were forever
changed by war and victims of violence everywhere.

Table of Contents

I.

FULCRUM POINT

We're only human, we say,
the spirit's weaker than the flesh
We are marred by imperfection
random thoughts block the light
undisciplined feelings block the thoughts
our bodies weaken our minds
our minds weaken our bodies
Yet when you think of the "I" of the astronomer
behind the eye of the Hubble telescope
looking back into time
across thirty orders of magnitude
perceptions aided by instrumental intelligences
to name and define quarks and quasars
moving the mind from the infinitesimal
to cosmic immensities
a miracle unfolds from where we stand
this very moment gazing
both inward and outward
simultaneously
Are we not the fulcrum point
of a zone of complexity
perfectly pitched on
the scales of time and space
where the universe is
awakening in
the blink of an eye?

AFTER MY TEACHER LEFT FOR CHINA
for George Venn, August 1981

Dry lightning flashes over Craig Mountain
Thunder crashes headlong through dense tamarack
Sun-split apples fall, bruised, juices sticky
and stale in the mouth of a bright-eyed yellow lab
Hot wind keeps the wistful journeyer on his sojourn
At the crossroads I cannot decide which way
to go so sit down in my brown grass
choked with weeds and speak to you
from where the storm has stalled, holding back
brief respite from the drought

How is the weather in Hunan, George?

Tu Fu squatted in your house
claiming the right as your other self
Alone in my study, I wonder, wouldn't the rule
of hospitality require then that he take
your place as *my* teacher?
From his example, I don't know which
is more important—finding patronage
or finding my own voice?
By now, he's plundered the hives
of their honeycomb and drank up the honey wine

Do your classes at the Railway Institute run on time?

Humming in and out of the roundhouse—
tick-tock, tick-tock—can you set your watch
by the regular intervals of students changing direction?
When they perform the miracle
of making light of it, do they pass around
forbidden mason jars filled with fireflies
in which they see each other's reflections?
I keep thinking if Tu Fu—drinking up the mead you left behind—
somehow reduces the world to a few good lines
would he only succeed in eliminating its body?

This I know:

we must let go our teachers
and let the world be our guide
Tu Fu doesn't keep his appointments
He passed out last night in your neglected garden
his voice lost in translation
somewhere between the Chinese cabbage and Oregon grape
I sit alone in the moonlight, severely sober
sidetracked on the road to anywhere
My words fall short but fall just the same
like first raindrops after a long hot spell

SNOWBALL AMBUSH

Dual-tracked, cross-eyed glare
of headlights catches me
marking progress post to post
in twilight trespass through
the neighbor's yard, snowball in my hand

The black knight races on, unblinking, unaware
He has claimed his tribute
taken the child from me again
I look for a chink in his crow-black armor
but no matter how I try

I always fail to stop him
The shiny black stallion races on
with the black knight crouching forward
pinning down the moon-eyed boy tossed over the saddle
I lead him just so, and this time *I know*

The release is smooth and natural
I hardly feel the cold compression
of resentment and rage
roll off my gloved fingers, shot
from a crossbow, straight to the mark
Even as slush from the horse's hooves
kicked up in my face blinds me
I see him wobble, fighting for balance
jerking at the reins, slipping in and out
of ruts, forced to drop the prize

Blurting like a quail
from behind a bare plum tree—
having delivered the blow anonymously—
I kneel in the snow to reclaim
the child I sell each day into slavery

The black knight will be back tomorrow
demanding tribute and I'll pay again and again
then in remorse on wet knees stiff and cold, freezing hands
barely able to hold intent, I'll wait for him at the edge
where his light is dim, where I don't have to give up
the child to be an adult

THE LAST EARTHBOUND ANNUNAKI
RELEASES A FALLEN ANGEL

There are others left behind who still believe in angels. We gather on moonless nights in dark living rooms, faces half-hidden in shadow, flickering in brief spasms of ritual light, not to plan a revolt but to drum, chant, throat-sing and recite from memory what we can only remember together.

Now and then we harmonize, our song rippling out in benign contagion to sift dust and detritus from the remains of what was built before, ringing deserted temples with blunt clappers.

From where they wait in their dispassion, high above the stricken armor, untainted by mortal concerns, invested in big banks and accumulating wealth, minor gods walk through gated communities, marking time in lesser heaven, untouched by longing. They keep us under surveillance, while plotting our future as market mules who never tug too hard on the tether.

When was the last uprising on the feedlot? The prize beef squat on garnish putting on the pounds.

You carry the genes of galactic knights and those who walk with the aid of their hands, your bones are made of both stardust and testosterone, now worth so-much-a-pound, left behind among the poorly evolved, cut-off from all beyond this world, no longer open to broadcasts from the stars.

You live on the earth now, safe within your orbit, spinning on your axis, tilting toward the sun. What is native in you infiltrates the flesh with phobias and flaws, viruses and vices, lays down roots over uneven ground even as your bruised knuckles part drifting continents.

The feats of still living heroes pass into legend. You listen for voices in the wind, unable to verify the vague generic prophesies channeled complete with ultimatums through unqualified receivers who never even graduated from mystery school.

When the missionaries they send down don't return, they send others, their eagle-eyes crossing like headlights, minds shuttered from all but black and white.

There must be billions of us left stunned and blinking, blinded by their artifice, yet mere millions who learn to dress in layers and curate the moon in their eyes, holding communion in dark living rooms to cobble together a fragile ground out of the moving morass of paradox.

You had to let her go. She will come back one day, you keep telling yourself, sitting on the edge of an unmade bed in a blue motel somewhere off the lost highway, having taken an off-ramp that never leads back on. The cheap painting of a seascape fades into the wall, its waves stilled at the breaking point in muted moonlight. Dreams like shadows fall into their objects. All you have left after her frantic flutter is the impossible impression of a trapped bird embossed on a double-paned window.

GIVING IT AWAY

I never told you this before
but those sanctimonious lectures
about holding onto your integrity
and refusing to sell out—
all bullshit!

Here's the truth:
I tried to sell my soul
repeatedly
but times are tough and the devil
can afford to be choosy

It was carefully packaged
formatted according to guidelines and sent
first-class to all the top agents—
those fastidious middlemen
in sharkskin suits cruising in BMWs
cellphones growing out of their ears
plucking blackberries in a jam—
but in the hands of those more intimate
with the devil, who knew his needs
what he was looking for
how much he was paying
my soul only suffered

And it always came back
sometimes with coffee stains
rumpled and torn
as if it had been slept with
even worse—sometimes unopened

Nothing kills the *animus spiritus* like leaving it
lay around, expecting to be supported,
watching daytime t.v.
hoarding its secrets
peeking from behind curtained windows

Used to be a well-used soul
retained some value like a fine leather sofa
the more cracked and worn
the better the fit
Or a battered steamer trunk
that's been around the world
with stickers from Bali, Burma and British Honduras
filled with forgotten moments dressed up
in exotic silks and old uniforms
Or a less-than-pure image polished and bid up
by a publicist with paid-for testimonials
after livin' it up, drinking imported beer
fucking like a rockstar

When goatboy came to collect
he found you so obese from debauchery
you could feed the fires for eternity
without spending all your fuel

So what if I limited myself
to the living room of my mind
without exploring attic or basement?
Sacrificed pleasures of the flesh
for the straight and narrow
only to end up in hell anyway?

Better to live my way down
than ascend with eyes closed
When I die, don't close my eyes
I want to see where I'm going
and if my soul's of so little value
that I'm going to have to give it away
it might as well be in poems

LET 'ER BUCK
At The Pendleton Round-Up

I lie breathless on my back
knight without armor
in ritual dance of man and nature

to dominate the nature of man
Sledgehammers bruise the soft meat
inside a cage of bone

I catch my breath
find my feet , dust off my hat
against the thickness of my thigh

No thrill in an easy ride
Tomorrow night
I'll stick longer

ride that bronc into hell
ride the wild tame
earn the name *buckaroo*

The pick up rider hooks my arm
slings me up breezy behind him
wheezy and wincing on his spooky appaloosa

I raise my arm
The crowd cheers
Some cheer

for the broken buckaroo
with the bruised ego
Some for the beast unbroken

FROM THE BLIND SIDE OF
FAILING STRUCTURES

So do we give up hammers, throw out building codes
settle for a house made of straw
a hot coal smoldering, keeping
the fire inside barely alive?
The heat is turned down so low
marrow freezes in the bone for fear
we'll burn the whole house down
It took everything we had to create even this
a left-handed off-centered world with built-in wobble
at its core, yet took no time at all to divide it
You may wonder what to do now with
your half of this temple to the temporary
this monument to mediocrity
this pedestal dedicated to impermanence
this pit of stale longing
The house was never perfect
Taking up the plumb bulb
we can find no true center
nothing level
nothing square
We never knew who left the trunks in the attic
or left behind the shadows we sewed to our feet
or ever used the tools in the toolbox under the stairs
or bothered to find out how they might set us straight
Small wonder we live in the shambles of disrepair

Can we ever be secure knowing
how many doors were left unopened?
How many dimensions left unexplored?
Our awkward shadows wobble away
knocked off their axis
smoldering in the moonlight
dragging us behind by the feet
hugging too little heat to conflagrate
worried maybe someday lightning *will* strike

UNHEARD CONCERT
OR DEAD ROCK STARS RETURN ON A GHOST PLANE

It isn't an easy landing. They miss the runway entirely. No one hears the crash. On the threshold of the sprung door a half-naked Door screams *"jettisoned in mute nostril agony..."* and leaps, eyes closed, down the chute in a puff of smoke. A soft croon that could be mistaken for a moan arises weakly resurrected in the back of the plane. Frankie staggers out, black bowtie unhitched, rubbing his eyes. Looking over black horn-rimmed glasses, Buddy hollars, "Didn't you get on the wrong plane?" "What happened to the Rat Pack?" Frankie croons-moans, sitting down on a flat rock, hands in his head feeling for the last of anything profound left from profound memory loss. A desert wood rat climbs up the rock, whiskers twitching, and lays down an offering of bones. "I said Ratpack, not Pack Rat," Frankie cries, smashing an empty bottle against the weak beam of a landing light. Behind him white blues, hair in flames, belches fire like a dragon. She offers Frankie her bottle and hotly blows into his ear, "Honey, here, have a drink. Maybe it'll help you remember." "How far are we from the Strip?" Frankie asks. "I don't remember getting on a plane. Sammy and Dino are waiting at The Sands." With neon butterflies detonating from his Afro and blinking out in a riff of stiff wind, Jimi exhales Purple Haze. Morrison, now totally naked, runs off into new moon madness, accompanied by howling coyotes. The soft-spoken Nashville boy, missing the splendid chaos of the living and finding no frenzied fans waving lighters in the air to keep his spirit alive, pulls his superhero cape over his head. "I told you to turn left, you simpleton!" Janis shouts at him. "It was on autopilot," the King mutters under his cape. Squinting at a strange sky filled with stars he no longer recognizes, Frankie suddenly starts, pointing toward a diffuse crown of light on the horizon, "Look," he says, "The Sands." And so it is. Sand and more sand. Sand and more sand.

THE OWL, THE GOLDEN EAGLE AND
THE BRISTLECONE PINE
A Najavo Story Thrice Retold

Owl perches on top of a tall pine, his head revolving as only Owl's can. "Look what I can do," he boasts, looking across the ridges and pinnacles that divide the Great Basin from the Colorado River drainage. His big round eyes take in vistas of red lands in the swivel of his head. Golden Eagle flies down from a hoodoo and settles on a pine tree. He folds his great wings and cocks his head, regarding Owl critically. He is unimpressed. Owl's sight takes in everything under the horizon, but still he has no vision. Owl revolves his head almost full round. "Look what I can do, look what I can do." Golden Eagle shakes his sharp beak. He is growing tired of Owl's silly arrogance. "Look what I can do, look what I can do," Owl boasts, head revolving like a beacon. Finally Golden Eagle has heard enough. "So what!" he cries, biting off the words impatiently. He sinks his talons into the top of the pine and spreads his wings, each wingbeat a thunderclap stirring up dust devils. Like ancient drums they echo down dry ravines, through hoodoos and over mesas. Prairie Dog and Badger cover their ears and dive into their burrows. Golden Eagle rotates up and up in a tight spiral, grasping the tree's crown in his talons. The strong pine holds its ground but Golden Eagle's powerful torque twists the trunk of the tree. Golden Eagle flies from pine to pine twisting them into cork-screws until they stagger over the red canyons. Owl's eyes get bigger and bigger, becoming bright full moons. Golden Eagle settles onto a hoodoo, folds his wings, squints at Owl and says, "Look what I can do."

LEGACY FOR BEACHCOMBERS
Rockaway Beach, for Sue

At sunset, with white hot tongues
of galvanized ten gauge boiling from the mouth
of a furnace forging steel, we are gulled
by unspoken regrets into thinking half-buried
rocks in luster of last light are enchanted

every hunk of pitted ground glass a precious
gem with which to repeal the missteps
and mistakes shot like rockets into the sky, bursting
and falling back with stardust into our arms

Between us, we walk off with one jagged piece
of might-be agate through which the sun unknots
memory from our muscles, unwinding
a spiral stair we climb out of ourselves, glass eyes
strung around our necks through which we look back

Convinced we're more mature
and discerning in this altitude when it comes
to what attracts our mountain-misted eyes
than thirty years ago when first we combed this beach

more mature and not so easily agape
as when we dragged plastic bags of unvetted
broken shells and rocks still glistening wet
with potential as pendent or amulet

when simple objects reclaimed with twilight's magic
were dropped into the crucible of our practice
philosopher's stone long since dried out dull
and ordinary, forgotten in peanut butter jars
on a shelf in our garage

Our eyes now are so filled with light
we cannot see what lies at our feet
We walk over whole worlds lying
silent, awash in the sheen of ebbing
tides following a mirrored sun

There are more agates on the beach today
than were there yesterday
We put them all back
for you to find

KILLING THE MONSTERS

The doorchime won't stop ringing
so I pull back the shade and stand
Pleistoscene blue eye to Precambrian black eye
with three generations of knee-less, odd-toed
one-ton ungulates standing on my front porch
The largest is southern white who blurs his words
with an indecipherable drawl, pushing the others
aside, intent on getting into my house
His critically endangered horn
made of pure keratin whose weight is worth
more on the black market than gold
presses relentlessly against my alarm
never letting up, refusing to leave

The smaller Sumatran is dull-eyed as an alligator
with half-masticated leaves in green drivel
submersing my welcome mat in a thick slime
I do not have a room big enough to conceal them
so I threaten to call the cops
Though I closed my door on the killing
in hopes the killing would stop
it only came farther down our street
I tried writing letters of protest
donated to causes for our protection, their protection
to keep them from going the way of grizzly or bison
But I did not invite them here
butting heads on my front porch
chuffing so hard the beams
of my house shudder

I'm aware of a certain dignity in their survival
that grotesquery is not skin-deep
that their sad complexion is not infectious
but they do not belong in my neighborhood
The poachers herded them into the box canyon
of our cul-de-sac for easy slaughter
turning us against them, calling them monsters
when they overturned our SUVs looking for somewhere to hide
The neighbors brought out their guns
and started blasting away
I'll say this: my neighbors aren't evil
but they believe people come first
They grow old and need better medicine
They need care and comfort
For the most part, it's a credit to them
that they've resisted so long
the temptation to kill their pain
by killing all the monsters
But time is running out, their eyes are getting bad
and they can't see who the monsters are

GREAT BLUE AT DUSK
Nehalem Bay, August 5, 2006

She's a still-life watercolor
on the dock of the Paradise Cove marina
balancing on one leg
Undistracted by sunset-feathered
silhouettes skimming the open windows
of her unwinking eyes, she waits—
all night if necessary—for the gift to rise
While twilight sorcerers skulk under veil of mist
in search of black magic
following rituals and spells down
shaggy canyons of coastal range
along rushing white water
her downcast eyes penetrate a deeper place
where flash of self rises through reflection
spreading its faint ripple

If only I could be such a study
in stillness and concentration
If only I could grasp the small stirring
before it's snapped up by these scissor-tails
cartwheeling in air with daylight's slow decay
While Herring gulls nod off
beaks laid back onto gray shoulders
she remains poised, unruffled,
a stoop-shouldered Groucho Marx
with thick brows pitched
to an inward gaze to stop time

No degree is necessary
to study this change of light
and the art of being still
is an act of vanishing
not by being reduced to nothing
but by expanding into everything
And what she does might be called conjuring
the result of some Great Blue magic
but I think instead it's reward
for attention to small things
and practice, most definitely
lots of practice

II.

WHERE THE YELLOW BRICK ROAD TURNS WEST

FOR MY MOTHER, MARY

"Find yourself a place where there isn't any trouble."
— Auntie Em

1.

Each day my new father led me
farther out and away from my sequester

in the warmth of your kitchen—
the one unassailable domain of women in those days

Sitting cross-legged in dubious sanctum under the table
with green plastic soldiers lined up to save the king

secured amid aromas of fresh baked bread
and the sound of eggs popping in bacon grease

I lived for the sweet privilege of licking rubber spatulas
thick with icing, my limbs laden with lard

from your biscuits and gravy, scalloped potatoes, hamburger casseroles,
macaroni and cheese, liver and onions, cornbread and chili

Did you worry then, mother, about the unforgiving nature
of a child playing God when I wiped out a whole platoon

with a single backhand, accompanied by a score of sound effects
from lip-sputtering explosions to blood-curdling battlecries and death throes?

Did you pray then as you spooned Hungarian goulash into the crockery bowl
Dear Lord, do not let my son grow up to be his father?

And did you want to cry all those times you chased me into a corner
wagging your shoe at wit's end because I asked for it?

because the scab of former life was still fresh enough to pick
and I kept picking at it until it bled?

because I couldn't understand how once you learn his name
even a God-fearing Christian woman can learn to live with the devil?

and maybe I blamed you just a little for believing
some benevolent power would protect the castle

I re-live the story in my mind as if I'd witnessed it myself
how our neighbor in Grand Rapids, Michigan, the gentle widower,

was shot on his stairs one night after helping us escape across town
how my father, blood of my blood, a disabled veteran,

trained as a sniper during the war, lay in wait, his rage
made righteous by another man interfering with his family

I imagine him waiting in the attic, Bible in his lap, a box of ammo at his side
and as that good man, whose name I forget, mounted the stairs

to his house that night, a single step in a split second saved him
from the fatal shot intended for his head

when blood of my blood pulled the trigger and the bullet flew
from the muzzle of the 30-30, wounding him in the shoulder

and I imagine him leaning heavily, weak with shock,
against his weeping 7-year-old daughter

baptizing her with his blood and I felt both guilty
and thankful at the same time because it was his blood, mother,

and the terror in that little girl's eyes that made you realize
"across town" would never be far enough

so you took my sister and I and fled to the end of the earth
to someplace he'd never follow, to a whole new world

2.

We were saved by a man who'd given up on God
and didn't much believe in any Promised Land

who found the God in you enough to sustain him for
the rest of his life and he brought his new family

to this fortress of solitude, a small ranch-house
with a generator, sweltering in the shade of cottonwood

It was as far from any paved road as from
your dream of an all-electric home

You could see any intruder on the leading edge of a dustcloud
slicing down that desert road a good mile away

No one would find us here
There would be no surprises

The ranch-house was surrounded by a moat of green pasture
under constant siege from an ever-expanding wasteland

of sagebrush and salt flats, the end of the world
within walking distance of our back stoop

Decades of porous antlers and faded license plates
adorned the side of the barn, its history

lost on me as we blew in
dragging our ghosts

Settling into this last retreat
we were thankful to put the past behind us

The distant blue mountains of the Snake Range hovered in a dry haze
where the Pleistocene lapping of Lake Bonneville waves

are forever embossed in fossiliferous limestone not far
from the Utah border just off the loneliest road in America

Even as we learned to spell our new last name
counting humps in the double "m" which rolled

on and on like the arid foothills, my new father
sensed my need for territory so each day

led me out and away to face my fears
to gain confidence enough to take

those first steps alone building forts out of haystacks,
climbing into lofts, hiding in stalls, riding the buckskin

bareback out to fetch Clara, our only milkcow,
steering the red John Deere while he tossed hay to the cattle

3.

The wide world seemed smaller then
and looking back now is like looking through a microscope

all the many details overwhelming their connections
and I wonder how I failed to understand that vast barren landscape

was killing some part of you, mother,
I would never know

I hadn't the wildest guess why
you'd grown so large that winter

Thinking maybe you'd packed on pounds to insulate
against the unrelenting wind on those winter nights

like the extra fat and fur packed on the bones of Herefords
to help them survive the unforgiving nature of a land more

Yahweh than Christ, not knowing what it took out of you
But you never complained, never let on

with the umbilical of family and friends severed
with only a holiday rendezvous with other ranchwives for respite

chattering together in the kitchen, thumbing through a catalog
of wishes while your men performed surgery on trucks and tractors

4.

Our former life on Belmont in Grand Rapids was not any picture
of domestic bliss, but a thin façade concealing an impaired patriarchy

Cheap textured tarpaper on the house was made
to look like brownstone and the Easter Sunday dress-ups

were intended as portraits of a perfect postwar family
Onward Christian soldiers marching on the road to progress

all the way to the New Jerusalem, God's Kingdom on earth
But stripped of illusion, the simple truth was:

I was never descended from kings
though named after one —

Israel's beloved slayer of Goliath, defender of God's law,
author of Psalms, who like this country was not without fault

I credit no king for planting my seed as what king
would backhand his wife for backtalk?

or stand so ready to sacrifice his son rather than control
an unforgiving nature more Yahweh than Christ

who begged to be forgiven time after time
but couldn't ever admit he was wrong?

I pray, dear Lord, that if I don't know when I'm wrong
that I will at least be man enough to listen to those who do

5.

The gradual changes of your pregnancy
were lost on me, mother, in eastern Nevada, 1956

until we visited my brother's grave
in Ely that day in early spring

The nature of sex was still unknown to me,
a mystery like the strange allure of Betty Boop

or the dreams and fantasies about the young teacher
with soft blue eyes who made me

take off my pants because the cuffs got wet
in a mud puddle on the way to school

and she sat me down in my underpants
behind a blackboard where only she could watch

but if I'd known then, mother, what you spared me
my desert Eden would have transformed into a wild

and dangerous place where bone black wolves
in trespass lap up bad blood and howl at the moon

where some part of you is forever buried alone
with only a small brass plate to identify him

6.

I was eight years old
with a new father, living in a new land

a harsh new land full of faults, its rocky crust
fractured high and low, with no outlet to the sea

It was a man's world where life and death
could not be hidden like the scars of earlier life

scars covered with makeup,
scars that stretched all the way back

to Brother Floyd, a man more Yahweh than Christ, blood of my blood,
who rattled our world from the epicenter of God's House

whose every word echoed like a canon
with *Thou Shalt **Not*** written in stone

a man whose best lessons were taught with the back
of his hand until we were saved by a man self-confessedly Godless

I hadn't really noticed, mother, what was growing inside you
as in the quiet of my room I turned a flashlight to my own warped space

praying each night I would not become my father
that nowhere in me would the slow accretion of hurt

and rage accumulate like calcium carbonate
forming in the recesses of Lehman Caves, stalactites and stalagmites

festering quietly in the darkness there, strange formations
of drip and flow that could one day cripple me

and people would say "like father like son" "blood is thicker than water"—
let them instead wonder how all that woundedness

turned into something so miraculous like the stone
draperies, parachutes and gothic palaces sculpted

invisibly in dark chambers deep inside sacred caves
secret places where spelunking warriors with torches

of twisted creosote dragged their dead
into the farthest narrowing corner of the underworld

crawling on red bellies abraded by green limestone
coming out into daylight

with thousands of years of relations like dust
in their hair, generations of stories repeated by the wind

singing in their eyes and whispering from their every step
and though I did not have the ears to hear

I somehow understood even then you can take the girl
out of Indiana but you can't take Indiana out of the girl

Over the years, I have learned to commit in faith that Spirit lives
in bristlecone and hemp, coyote and hare,

that there is God in the gopher and God in the gopher snake,
God in the ground squirrel and God in the hawk

and I realize, mother, though you brought God with you
into this desert you couldn't bring along the whole Church

7.

After days on the road half-sick on exhaust in the back
of a Greyhound we disembarked into a dreamland, my Oz,

standing disoriented on a tile mosaic of the head of a Hereford bull
in the lobby of the Stockmen's Hotel in Elko

The Wild West was somewhere between Pecos Bill and Paul Bunyan,
and everywhere just around the bend were grizzlies and rattlers

renegades wearing warbonnets riding bareback
and a plain pine box displaying a dead man leaning against a barber pole

It was out there just over the rise with real cowboys like John Wayne
cowboys in cowboy boots and cowboy hats

with silver buckles pinching hardrock bellies
and tanned leather faces with watering eyes squinting

through Camel smoke as they set cherries and lemons
to spinning against all odds, whooping and hollering

as alarms sounded and slot machines disgorged a sluice
of silver dollars, their hands black from dirty money

My mother took a job as a motel maid and at the El Rancho
met the man behind the curtain who would raise me

and after a short stay in central Utah amid Mormon relatives
so avid in their genealogy you saw them as

badgers digging into the roots of your family tree,
we soon found ourselves in the total immersion

of an Old Testament story of isolation and self-reliance
on the Hawthorne cattle ranch

8.

As a boy in 1956 my sense of geography
extended no farther than the eye could see

What I could not see was more myth than map
so I imagined a Midwest tornado had ripped through our Michigan home

and dropped me into the desert long before
it ever reached the Land of Oz

The Hawthorne ranch was a world unto itself
like a remote island surrounded by a sea of sage

and I was its prince, son of the rightful king
who lost his kingdom to the lord of the underworld

The king had been banished to a far away land to subsist
like a monk in a beehive cell eating fish and bread

and on those days the son hurting from his absence followed
the good knight out into the fields like a squire learning

to keep the land alive, opening and closing water gates
using a spade to redirect the flow into green pastures

peeling a sharp eye for black snakes, beheading them
with one quick downward thrust of the gleaming shovel blade

unquestioned judge and executioner
in defense of home defense of family

and though the afternoon sun baked
all the energy from my body and drops of sweat

striking the ground failed to turn
the cement hard alkali flats into beanstalks

I still believed tomorrow would be a better day
because, mother, you had given me this

because you never gave up on miracles
because being here was miracle enough

9.

I found the miracles only
after I'd given up on them

It was a miracle that I could whistle back
the black and white spotted shepherd dog named "Spot"

when he chased the wayward sheep back
over the hill, nipping their heels

We ran together from pasture to corral to barn
and it was a miracle he remained my best friend after cuffing

his ears for coming home smelling of skunk and kicking him
for chewing up a green plastic bazooka man

You waited, mother, your whole life, for a miracle
waiting to witness Jehovah's parting of the Red Sea

but missing every day on the ranch
miracles of adaptation and resiliency

like the kangaroo rat that can go its entire life
without drinking water or the spadefoot toad

that burrows into the soil and goes dormant
until vibrations of rain striking the ground awaken it

Miracles happened every day there
Yet if I'd known then what I know now, mother,

instead of the Promised Land—with one-room schoolhouse
glowing in morning light, white and drenched with sun

visible on the rise from the back stoop
across green pastures of flood-irrigated grazing grass

where during lunch I chased dun lizards
through twisted greasewood and bombed cottonwood leaf boats

in the rocky creek with round white stones—
I might have been driven to the brink of breakdown

unable to go on living in that desert under
the relentless assault of wind and dust

going crazy like the wives of farmers
on the Plains during The Great Depression,

women pulling out fistfuls of hair
as angry nature came howling

under doors, around windows,
the walls of their homes so permeable

that even the chambers of their hearts filled up
with sand, their blood vessels turning to stone

10.

I can only guess how my center, my Eden,
for you, mother, a good Christian woman thrown into this desert

for God's own cruel amusement, left on the side of the road
in an overheated Pontiac Chiefain with busted radiator

miles from any garage, dust plume settling on the seat,
on your clothes, on your eyelashes, while you waited for your new husband

to return with water enough to get us to Ely in time,
must have been like waking up on the Plains of Armageddon

between forces of good and evil poised
to contest for your baby's soul

You kept praying for miracles, over and over striking
your Aaron's rod against red rock though no water came

no ravenous seagulls flocked over the hill
to devour the locusts

You always worried too much and lived too little
saving us from the truth, bearing up with a weak smile

when lost in nowhere surrounded by nothingness
when all around the spare sage-mottled hills

backed by imposing barriers of mountains
dark with piñon pine and deep ravines

the hard facts of daily life tested your faith
threatening to defeat any promise of another world

"After all I've been through," you once said, "there'd better be a heaven
and I'd better not find any mansions or I'm gonna burn 'em all down

because if heaven is nothing more than a duplication
of what I've found on earth I'll be damned."

When I finally stopped long enough to ponder heaven
I had to wonder why that vastness was so empty some nights

then on others in all its glory full of stars bright and reeling
the full moon tethered round and white like a balloon

and I stood like Dorothy clicking her heels
looking up, dumbfounded

as it floated there just beyond my reach
big as your belly

11.

That fall my older sister and I found a litter of kittens
birthed in haystacks and by the scruff of their necks

pulled them out one by one and my black Midnight
got into the spring house and gorged himself

to death on rich cream and I learned
to be wary of too much of a good thing

Every day I walked through a pasture
to go fetch our only milkcow for milking

passing through a small herd of mustangs
they'd rounded up to remove them from the range

One morning father lifted me up onto Buck's
bare back and said I was no longer to go on foot

That buckskin gelding's cropped black mane was stiffer
than the bristles on a hairbrush and combed my hands

before I latched on, digging my heels into his flanks
and trotting past those snorting steeds

stamping their hoofs, ripping up the sod
their eyes wild and full of devil's fire

Inside the barn a solitary silent owl
hunched in the darkest corner, betrayed only by

white droppings on the rusted horseshoe
nailed upside down above the barndoor

so our luck wouldn't run out
letting the past catch up with us

Even though I couldn't see that barn owl
up in the rafters I always knew he was there

and I'd start talking to him
as soon as I entered the darkness

12.

The only gas stop between Baker and Ely had these bubble-headed
lighthouse-looking pumps—the kind where the gas

flushes to the top then goes down as it gurgles into your tank—
and their Payday candybars were thick as my arms

and you could easily save half for later
in case the car broke down

We drove past the junction for Lehman Caves
in our '52 Pontiac stationwagon

up over Connors Pass to visit you in the hospital
but they wouldn't let children into your room

So we stood on new grass below your window and waited
for you to appear in white gown, waving wanly from the second story

Stricken thin and phantom pale
that image haunted me for years

though I hardly ever thought about the little brother
whose whole life spanned only a few hours

My sister, Judy, and I believed God would punish us
for anything less than total devotion

"God doesn't welcome lukewarms into His House,"
the preacher at the First Assembly of God in Grand Rapids

warned in a voice more Yahweh than Christ
and all us lukewarms stared at our shoes

waiting to be snatched from the pews and dragged
down into the fiery pit of hell and damnation

Disaster struck outside me as a boy
though it struck and struck often

sometimes so close I could feel the hair
prickle on the back of my neck

like the sudden drop in air pressure, the sick stillness
you feel in your stomach before the tornado hits

Life was miracle followed by tragedy
that's just the way it was

God was an insensitive brute
impersonal as an earthquake or a flashflood or a lightning strike

I never saw much compassion in Him
We weren't even supposed to pray for ourselves

So what do you do with all this unexpressed love and anger
between Father and Son and all this history that leaves out

a crucial part of the Trinity—our mother Mary
who came to resemble the Holy Ghost?

My own Godlike arrogance took hold of a sturdy stick
to provoke dumb confusion in a hill of red ants

so it seemed only natural that our whole lives
would be stirred up by really nothing personal

13.

We'd already lost one home to an angry nature
and it would be years before I learned

some disasters you carry around
rot from the inside out

creating twisted black cavities
hardening into boils

sores you hide with long-sleeved shirts
sores that won't go away until pinched open

healing over into cratered scars
on adolescent skin

On February mornings in muck up to our knees
my new father and I held our vigil until blood-slick calves

dropped into melting drifts and we watched the cow
lick them clean, watched them wobble

to their feet and find a teat
Though believing we were in control

our job was mostly to witness the miracle
without intervention

But I also remember, mother, the heifer
too deep in mud to move

She worked herself into that suckhole
up to her chest, head and tail

thrashing all morning until she expired
in the heat of the afternoon

You watched from behind the screen door
shading your eyes as I raced astride the buckskin

to fetch father from the fields to rescue that cow
from Yahweh's terrible hunger, knowing in my heart

the Old God must still be angry
angry maybe because I turned against my father

angry maybe for my loving the earth too much
and losing sight of heaven

We didn't know how a hard knot on the family tree
was growing heavier in you by the day, mother,

hardening like a boil, hunching you over
with dead weight and how the sky

was suddenly empty of moon when my brother
went from the womb to the grave

14.

We found the slim history of life before father
pressed into a single photo album

buried deep in the back of your closet
The Gordian knot was cut

Long-held enigmas were unraveled like why
you protested so heatedly when our Mormon relatives

used genealogical research to invade your privacy
like when Judy, at fifteen, found you crying

over a letter from Florida
holding a news clipping in your hand

like the black and white photo of you with an un-named man
wearing a fine suit and immaculate shoes

kneeling beside a stroller with a baby we couldn't identify
Was this proof of another life in hushed dormancy for years

closely guarded and undisclosed until
congestive heart failure took you from us?

Going through your things in the apartment in St. George
we found the clipping about my drowned half-brother

making some sense of my own fear of water
underscored by my nearly drowning at about the same time

falling into the deep end of the pool at a swimming party
for the baseball team because I wouldn't admit I didn't know how to swim

Your first marriage ended when his rich family
in Florida decided some barefoot Indiana farm girl

was simply not worthy of their son
but bearing down long enough to endure the pain

you gave birth to a new beginning
with another man, blood of my blood, whose angry nature

burned a brand onto my heart and I remember how
he tore me from your arms at the bus station

He was on the run after shooting the widower
and they caught him, returned me to you

and he was led away, hands shackled behind his back
revolving red lights atop the police cruiser screaming at me

and the policeman's hand on his head
firmly guiding him down into

the dark backseat of the black and white
on that day when the whole world turned gray

15.

Hurry, dad, I cried, *something's wrong*
The-only-man-I-ever-knew-as-father

wheeled the John Deere through
deep ruts in the access road

bouncing the haywagon's balloon tires over blackheads
of blunt rock breaking out on the earth's tawny skin

coiled rope and harness dancing in the bed
Come quick! I cried astride the gelded buckskin

In the pasture, the wild horses snorted and stared
my intrusion catching them napping on their feet

waking with nostrils flared in midday heat as I galloped by
cutting spring-sprung grass like a scythe

kicking up the sod against the fenceline
Father, come quick! You gotta do something!

but before the men could measure her fix
that heifer gave up, no fight left

her heavy tongue unscrolled through a froth
Dad called the neighbor to winch her up

and render her down, the shaggy red hide
put to soak in a 40-gallon drum

So this is what it comes to:
my childhood paradise was your prison

and I couldn't see far enough beyond myself
to know what you went through that winter

You wiped the fog of your breath from the cold window
with the sleeve of your tattered housecoat

wrapped in a green army blanket
crouched over the oil stove

to keep warm as the stiff Nevada wind
wolfed through thin walls

nipping your heels
knocking you down inch by inch

and as you gazed beyond the dust devils and whirling snow
in the front yard to far-away places beyond the brittle sundown

to a land of never was where
you guarded your secrets in solitude

the power failed and the generator ran out of gas
your image flickered like an old-time movie

and I saw then for the first time that part of you—
uprooted with the failing foundation of marriage and home

a tumbleweed hung up on barbed wire
a shadow in the mist sustained by a kildeer's cry

a haunting dissonance settling over the breaks
climbing out of bed and slapping the cold floor

with bare feet, waking up alone
in the dark like a silent owl in the rafters

16.

The good Mormon doctor awaited word from the eldest son
Unplug the heart and lung machine

It's the right thing to do
You'll never come out of the coma

The tears in your eyes, he assured me, were a biological
response—nothing more, nothing less

Your mind was gone, he said
You couldn't hear us talking

You'd suffered stroke after stroke during the night
that blackest of nights, the sky empty of stars

the moon just a sliver of light
sadly on the wane
So I gave the word and let you go
and by the time the family albums finally passed to me

the photos and clippings with news of my drowned half-brother
were gone, maybe lost in the fire that gutted my sister's home

though I sit now with boxes of photos and memories
stacking and sorting them as best I can to separate

black and white
from color

truth from
half-truth

and with you and dad gone
and two brothers and a sister already in graves

I wonder how much of this history
is more myth than map?

how much is public record?
how much would you prefer I keep private?

I forgive you, mother, for your secrets
and hope you will forgive me

if I cannot promise
not to tell

III.

WHERE STATELY MANSIONS ONCE STOOD
After Hurricane Camille, Keesler AFB, June 1970

1.

Detoured single-lane on U.S. 90 to Gulfport,
the chartered Greyhound with new airmen
steers past flagmen around washed-out
highway in the hurricane disaster zone
Flung inland and left marooned on high ground
by the storm surge, a shrimpboat lists on broken keel
amid the sweet decay of inherited wealth
where stately mansions once stood

Just off the bus from basic, you march through slop,
another downpour, practicing to perform the tedious
without complaint, the faultless creases of pickle green fatigues
cutting the air in stride to chow hall in the predawn dark
They call you *skinhead,* the glorious tangles of
your "long beautiful hair" left in a pile
ankle-deep on the barber's floor at Lackland

You weren't in Biloxi when Camille hit—
a dark carnival blowing in on a midnight train
with strange calliope music, slugs of stiff wind
unfurling black tents, whirling round
an otherworldly eye of blue sky over Keesler
You are happy now to draw k.p. instead of cleanup detail
where those unranked and unlucky enough sift a mélange

of rubble and sand through fine-mesh screens for hazards
and anonymous bones, feeding fires with tons of debris
scoured from beaches still off-limits
seven months after landfall

2.

In the mess hall, air forces of West Germany,
South Korea, Holland and Cambodia watch their backs
hunched over chow—runny eggs and lukewarm sausage
in thickening grease, stacks of pancakes
with mounds of margarine melting in too much syrup
Unable to fend off the jack rabbits who snatch up
trays too long unattended, the Homebase boys come back
with dessert and coffee to find their place
at the table already cleared
 "Damn skinheads," they curse you
as you lean back against the wall keeping
your vigil, fighting to stay awake
after a late shift on hurricane watch

Blinded by flashlights after lights out
you were fooled into thinking folded tinfoil
was first lieutenant bars so followed orders to sit
on a wooden chair outside on the fire escape, hyperalert,
watching for hurricanes as the moon bobbed
like a whistle buoy
untethered by the storm

We snap to attention,
property of the U.S. government, names
stitched above the right pocket of our fatigues
stamped into the neck of your t-shirts
stenciled into the elastic of our boxers
We learn to spell with the military alphabet—
alpha, bravo, charlie, delta, echo—
learn to tell Greenwich Mean Time
to hand-print legible messages for the brass
calibrate ground radios to zero blindfolded
tune in the right frequencies
We are trained to handle simulated Maydays from memory
in strict accord with FCC regulations, to bounce
our voices off the underside of heaven
while never once getting off the ground

Ducking into the snackbar and out of a sudden cloudburst
on the way to laundry, you cool down with a tall Coke,
chewing on ice and mopping sweat from the back of your neck
listening to "American Woman" on the jutebox
The streets are overflowing one minute
then its 95 degrees with 98% humidity again
Lifer brats—hanging out another day without light,
smoking under-age—act out sad dramas
to withstand the test of tedium
like twisted trees with broken limbs
whipping dangerously across the room
caught in a storm they didn't create

drafted into a war they didn't begin
a war dead-ahead that will never end
so long as we let ourselves
become its instruments

LOST TRANSMISSIONS
MOUNTAIN HOME AIR FORCE BASE, 1971
FOR KENNETH D. PHARES

1.

Skylark Niner Niner, how do you read, over?

I read between the lines
grace notes lost in the margins
the unsaid unheard evaporating in air
like a mirage rippling over the desert
I hear Gabriel blow in the prairie grass
as the old world ends and a new one begins
Your mother's mourning brought me here
as our eyes met under a seven-gun salute
and I imagined she must wonder why
I should live and her son die
Guilt-driven to obsess over filling your shoes, my friend,
I made you perfect in my mind
too perfect perhaps to imitate
too perfect perhaps to be real
Your death inspired me to
either become the man
you might have been
or
the man I was meant to be

When you filed your flightplan
did you intend so warped a trajectory?
Did you fly off course

misled by your instruments?
To spare your brother, you joined the Marines
and they handed you a pocket Bible and an M-16
taught you to kill then flew you
directly from the Phillipines to Dong Ha
where you died in a mortar attack setting up camp
before you'd even unslung your rifle
Your death, Skylark, taught me to sing,
the voice coming from somewhere deeper
from the land of the dead
from the other side I found inside
I volunteered to become an airman, taking an oath
to support a war I didn't believe in—a war
you might have called "just"
an aggression to stop aggression
killing to stop killing
war to end war
Now I drive back and forth through sagebrush
duty-bound every day, battling boredom and the blues,
a half-obedient airman on a double-back shift
caught by the wedge between day and night
a radio operator running into my own transmissions
coming and going, crashing through catacombs
and caves crackling static on the airwaves

2.

Skylark Niner Niner, I say again, do you read, over?

I think maybe I'm not getting through to you
I've crashed in a desert
somewhere outside the margins of time
my guts churning from the reek
of slow rabbits baking in the sun
dead in a dull thud
insides unreeled by weight of my wheels
as I drive to the single-sideband station
Anything soft covered with fur or hard shell
fast or slow, high or low,
finds no sympathy here
no fitting monuments
for mind and memory
locked inside the men
locked inside the mechanical puppet
following orders, faithfully articulating
arms and legs, hands and feet
to create a monster that invades and occupies
a fiery dragon that bombs and strafes
following head instead of heart
giving over control to those
who should know better

3.

Skylark Niner Niner, please acknowledge, over?

What would you have me do?
In the fullest light and darkest night
shadows retreat into you
no longer visible, but still defiant and undefeated
You cannot kill them, cannot defeat them
so must learn to live between two pitiless masters
war and peace
God and country
right or wrong
War will never free us from darkness, Skylark;
it only drives the darkness deeper
where it doubles and redoubles in strength
Shouldn't we instead coax the darkness into light
to better see its face, to name it, call it out
if only long enough to find our humanity?
Sustained from shift to shift by eat and sleep
only to serve the State in killing the shadow
destroying some enemy
I wake after a wet dream
with salt-sore eyes searching for likeness
having skimmed lagoons so blue and clear
I see ancient shipwrecks decaying on the bottom

in a latitude where the depths are so deceiving
I forgo the bathysphere and dive naked
so far down combustible fish attach themselves
to my flesh and we come up too fast
in a silent scream spilling into my barracks room
the altered light of a capsized moon
I've become this lifeform so strange
as to be nameless as a whore
swimming back from the tropics of her hair
into blinking banks of conditions
my mouth unspooling
outage reports in triplicate
hands blue from pulling carbons
the soul loss so palpable I'm choking on it
Thunderbirds roll in sonic boom
skywriting in jetstreams a language
I cannot read
They will win this fight without us
but in winning they will be less constrained
the next time the war drum beats
These blood vows are slurred by ambivalent winds
blowing like Gabriel over a foreign country
And all I know or think I know
all I believe or think I believe
means nothing if made subordinate to duty
There is no honor in that

It's what the head does without the heart
I am not Samson swinging the jawbone of an ass
conscripted into a labyrinth not of his own making
I made a choice, took an oath, but the man
who took the oath is not the man I was meant to be
and the man I was meant to be must now break that oath
Therein lies my strength

Looking back from the perimeter across the flightline
a necklace of precious stones strung glittering
on the edge of silence, I remember when I first arrived on this desert
and Captain Nightingale who was a kamikaze during the war
climbed into his Phantom and strapped himself in
"You must learn to lean back slowly," he advised,
"'Cause it's a long way to fall
and you don't even know you're falling
until you've hit the ground"

4.

Skylark Niner Niner, why don't you answer, over?

As much as I click my heels and repeat to myself
There's no place like home
there's no place like home
I only need look outside the barracks window—to low clouds

beaching themselves like sick whales on the rounded foothills
listen for the toothless lion who cannot find his forest
so roars without will—to feel the grief for what we've lost
on those journeys we didn't want to take
the old worlds dying into new ones
our bags on the bus
our shadows falling behind
the terrible weight we drag
like an anchor we cannot cut loose
past men with no legs on the corner
blowing smoke signals we cannot read
How can we find our way home, Skylark,
when we never really had one?
So I say we say "here" is our home wherever we go
and wake each morning to a new world

WHEN THE WAR COMES HOME

When you win, you win for all
Dancing in the street with your lost self
When you lose, you lose alone
How it all ends remains to be seen

Dancing in the street with your lost self
When the war comes home
How it all ends remains to be seen
A ghost standing at attention behind your back

When the war comes home
She's afraid you might break in two
A ghost standing at attention behind your back
Afraid to touch the cracks

Afraid you might break in two
Walking wounded as you do
Afraid to touch the cracks
One foot in and one foot out

Walking wounded as you do
Day and night wearing a death mask
One foot in and one foot out
Caught between worlds here and there

Day and night wearing a death mask
Walking wounded, one foot in, one foot out
Caught between worlds here and there
She fears she cannot give enough to save you

Walking wounded, one foot in, one foot out
When the war comes home
She fears she cannot give enough to save you
You never really make it home again

You never really make it home again
Though you stand at ease and fall out
Even if you win, you lose
When the war comes home

THE GLASSBLOWER
For Tom Dimond

Looking into your glass paperweight
I gaze into a crystal skull
bursting with supernova
Time-compressed worlds within worlds
conceived in fire and fissured from
cold galaxial light, a bubble of breath,
thrown down from the highest mountains
by the thunder spirits, ballast for the hollow bones
of skittish flocks of words with wings
ready to take flight as hunters
hunker down with a warm gun
A sound rushing like wind through red willow
expelled in the crack of words, split by flames
into two halves like the moon
dark side hidden, light side, cold and sharp
cutting bolts of black velvet with starshine
My poorly-formed and aborted attempts
at transformation collide and shatter into new particles
blinking out before I can see myself in their light
My lungs empty and fill, empty and fill,
wheezing like punctured bellows
and from a hiccup the invisible becomes visible
the whole universe expanding, fogged over
by someone's breath

FANTASY ON BLACK ICE
A Love Song for My Muse

I step into the cold air this wintry night and my head
cracks open like a thunderegg, exposing clusters
of crystalline inactions perhaps forming in darkness for eons
Semi-conscious, driven by habit, I steer my Vista
through idling fleets of tractor trailers anchored in a storm
Both passes are closed, but the road home remains open

My experience in all that's exotic/erotic
is that of a peeper, a naughty boy copping a feel
in the balcony, not thinking about consequences
and never putting too much on the line
I'm a transient trained to get on and off love's highway
knowing just how many miles to the next exit
but here I am stewing in vain, caught in the headlights
like a stunned opossum in the middle of the road
awkward as a teenager fevered by a classy chassis,
robust horsepower revving as she rounds
the corner leaving messages for me to follow
Is it infidelity to be seduced by language?
Why shouldn't we touch and taste the world through words?
She offers this slice of honeydew, cold and firm,
holds it out for me to sniff then places it on my tongue
She takes my hand and leads me to ripe plums sloughed
onto wet ground and asks why I would just let them rot?
Peeling the delicate skin and pinching the flesh
so the sugar pools around a dark soft bruise
I imagine the pleasure more cultured fingertips
might possibly articulate on her skin, fingertips nimble
from turning pages of epics, playing Mozart on a baby grand,
fine-tuning the telescope to bring Venus into sharper focus

Is it obscene to want to nibble and suck the sweet juice
from the very one you're committed to?
My fingers are winter-stiff and clumsy
rough nails clipped to the nub
all numb and cracked from work and less likely to excite
I could be every other middle-aged male
lamenting the twilight of precious virility
looking forward to antidepressants and Viagara
Unschooled as I am in finer techniques
of tongue-and-groove or the machinations
of a steamfitter's hands threading pipe to exact standards,
not knowing how much force or leverage to bring to bear
on a rusted joint without breaking it clean off,
confused as I am about functions
of carpels and stamens, pistons and valves
I know a hard drive is totally useless
without compatible software
and that is why I turn to you even in my sleep

Trusting too much in my machine riding
over the same neglected stretches through sulfur fog
without touching the brakes around Hot Lake
where water blows onto the road and freezes
I skid mere inches from the guardrail,
up over the overpass down into the clear
long enough to see your lithe form in tiger stripes
lounging in a deckchair on a white sand beach in Baja,
sipping fruit liqueur and twirling a red paper parasol
between thumb and forefinger
We deserve this, you and I, a day together in paradise
for the years of unappreciated labor

for the home we've built a day at a time
for the love we've made and the comfort we find in it

I see your come-on eyes blinking in the sun
Warm waves lapping the tropical shore
polishing California Bubbles and Banded Tulips
Nature's lapidary wears round
the green soapstone and I rise
amid more shades of blue than Gauguin could name
The electric arc from the tips of my fingers
when I touch the light hairs
on your thighs recalls our first kiss
exploding my nerve endings and melting the cool core
under the mantle of my skin

Just as I brush your lips with mine
stranded drivers in canned sleepers wake;
dreams of muskmelon women in white lace
dissipate, Ladd Canyon opens and steamy cabs
roll out on chains picking up lively banter on CBs

Still cradled here coasting in neutral
along a dim road crossing the valley to Union
coming home to you
I hoard these sweet imaginings
but only for a moment
as black ice at Catherine Creek Bridge
always startles me
even with my mind on the road

ARMAGEDDON ON MONDAY NIGHT FOOTBALL

We can expect an epochal battle tonight, Howard, as two perennial powerhouses lock horns for the right to face the Oriental Express for world domination. It's an interesting matchup. The contrasts couldn't be starker. The Western Eagles will be looking to strike early through the air with the long bomb. This Eagle offense has loads of weapons to reduce the field to cinders but relies on a stingy defense to capitalize on mistakes made by the Mideast Oil Kings to maintain their advantage. You can count on the The Kings to crawl out from under a smoking rock undeterred. They will do what they do best, erase that Eagle advantage by wearing down their defense with a gut-busting, jaw-breaking ground game, the product of a well-drilled squad that will have to drill even deeper, tonight, to strike pay dirt. The Kings fullback, The Persian Knight, isn't afraid to bang heads with that Eagle line and something's gotta give. The clock may decide this one. Time of possession is key. If the Kings keep it close, that Eagle defense may run out of gas. Conditioning is everything this far into the season, and the staying power of the Eagle front line has been suspect in its last couple of crusades.

We're in the fourth period, folks, and this has been a head-knocker. These true-believers are killing each other. The Kings may have fewer weapons but have cut into that Eagle advantage with a simple but effectively improvised attack—straight up the middle with an explosive charge. It's a standoff of Biblical proportions.

Third and seven on the Eagle twenty-six. The Kings need to hold the field. Ahmed and The Persian Knight need more help from the Koran against these odds. Ahmed takes the snap and hands off to his power fullback.

The Persian Knight ducks under his mountainous right guard and finds a hole to hide in. It closes quickly, but that big offensive line compresses it into a black hole and rolls it over their opponents. The Knight gave up his body on that one, Howard. Everything depends on the sacred spot. They do a body count, clear the field of collateral damage and bring in the chains. But the chains are broken. The Kings are going for it! The Eagle line is playing with mouths open. "Praise Allah!" The Kings shout in their huddle, sensing an upset, waiting for a prayer to be sent in from Dubai.

Eagle's linebacker, Samson Samuel, has been hitting hard all day. What can you say about this guy? He's all heartland. He dances up to the line on a blitz then backs off, narrowing his eyes, setting The Kings' quarterback in his sights. Dead on his feet, Ahmed takes the snap. Oh, what a bone-jarring collision! He can't keep his head on. Samson mistakes it for a fumble, scoops it up and starts running the opposite direction, picking up blockers. The Persian Knight walks untouched into the endzone.

We're all even. One minute left. Through a cacophony of fundamental fandom, chanting and singing, trumpets and drumlines, human waves waving, Achilles Jones misfires blowing out a whole section in a desperate attempt to constrain these martyrs. In the waning seconds, he avoids a fierce rush, steps up to fill his pockets and throws a long bomb. A Hail Mary, three hail Marys, five hail Marys. Right into the endzone. Tall Timber Tillman from Oregon gets a hand on it, bobbles it. Oh, he can't hang on, Howard. It looks like we're going to *sudden death*.

EXORCISM
A Vietnam Veteran Gives Up the Ghost

When you first came back into the world
laying in ambush behind a blind, in the hush
of Ladd Marsh, you heard only the cries of wounded warriors
in every China pheasant you shot down

You stand ready to lock and load
as the silence is twisted into conspiracy
unseen infiltrators move between dimensions
and take on any shape or form

You once read death in the eyes of young Marines
so kept a safe distance to escape
the gravity of their deadfall
worrying about what they read in yours

If there was a God, He was driven
underground by saturation bombing
So now you keep your head down, resisting
dreamflights and avoiding groundshadows

but they always overrun your perimeter in the night
and you wake up pulling the trigger
until today here in the field
in a valley where the soil is deeper

than all the pain of the world's wars
Being alive suddenly makes sense
and you realize you can speak in tongues

a new language—
Wallowa
Imnaha
Wapiti
Cop Copi

Chinook
Kokanee
Finally you've found words
to live by

Flushed from high grass
heart thrumming in steep ascent
you break free, taking evasive action,
banking first left then right

The black flack
of survivor guilt never quite catches up
You blow by, leaving a world not chosen
spinning bellyup in the slipstream

and when you land in the cool shadows
of granddaddy cottonwood
your story climbs limb by limb
concealing no weapons

IF ORPHEUS HAD PLAYED THE SAX
FOR GREG JOHNSON

When the coal train jumped its track
the engine's indifference to the engineer
destroyed his home and family
and sent Orpheus searching underground
Roots absorbed dark crude
Trees sloughed their skins
walking dead upright, blight rising as through a derrick
The banks of rivers grew slick with disgust
Orpheus heard the deep undertone of the snake moan
guts twisting, black tongue
swollen in its throat
The world, he thought, must be ending

Orpheus watched his flesh and bones, stripped of its culture,
carried off in chains on slave ships, his joy entangled
with mirage dissolving in a heat wave
The first faint reckoning of a far-off tsunami
climbed onto the rocks like a lungfish barely breathing
its knotted internal rasp
absorbed into lynchings and crowns of barbed-wire
Orpheus picked up his roots and followed the echoes
to where the edge lost its meaning
where the veil between night and day
sleeping and waking
living and dead, grew as faint
as the light between beast and shadow

Orpheus was a broken radio that lost its music
full of static, twisted with wires and loose connections
ribs knocking together like vacuum tubes
At the edge where he lost his edge
Orpheus tuned his receiver to pick up the echoes
and was answered by another world
He turned down the volume of his speech
and from that day forward there came
this unlikely music
from an instrument that growled
aggressively, hot and hard, steeped
in the blood of his heart
striking away all chains

Look for Orpheus first through the body
riding a sound wave just under the skin
He has always been there
keeping the beat
From the firepit of a forgotten cave
that hasn't seen a torch for a thousand years
something from nothing is born
but not without a price
knocking down the silence
throwing the moon out of its orbit
like a ghost passing through stone walls
flickering alive with shamanic bison and bear

through the mouth of time
to tumble into a smoke-filled speak-easy
finding the G-spot on stage
where smoke rings blow through his axe
after every trespass and stolen kiss
runs the gauntlet between sense and sensation
just long enough to grant the wild traffic right of way
long enough to stop time in nine different dimensions
to still the supersonic bomber, bomb bay open,
from dropping its bombs, dangling from
its jetstream, arrested while breaking
the sound barrier

SOFT MUSIC
Remembering William Stafford

1.

He would say every voice matters

2.

Some are pyrotechnic displays
evoking *oohs* and *ahhs*
others whirling dervishes
samurai with swords
cutting to the quick

Still others are soft
sustained like water over rock
wind through pine
the sound of rain

Those in exile finally break out
run naked down the street
Those in offices dumbed down by policy
reduced to no more dimension than a flag
gasp and wheeze at every extreme
declare all others
dangerous

3..

You can relax into his soft music
as into a chorus of crickets

on a summer night
faint stars dusting down the lilac
with a subtle light

4.

Those voices reduced to rant
crying out loud
may make us   twitch

                                             squirm
                                             back away
                                             blinking, dazed
stalled on the threshold
        where we glimpse the human heart silently retreating

5.

Who would expect to find such power
in a felt hammer striking piano strings
in the sounding of a Tibetan singing bowl
the vibrations ringing your bones
deepening your breath, expanding
ripples on still water where volume
does not equal distance?

6.

He teaches us to always cast deep
for whatever we reel to the surface

dark, wet and writhing, is our relative
in a different light not nearly so threatening
if we maintain a relative position

7.

Turning to face fierce eyes in the dark
we measure their light
judge their nature and intent
by first cracking them open
with soft music

8.

He'd say you need not raise your voice
        so much as find it

9.

You may not hear him in these lines
        for he speaks through the silences
at the summit of a forest road in midwinter
where you pause on cross-country skis
when the ocean inhales after the spent wave

I'm learning to be more patient
learning I don't need to knock down walls with hammers
so much as sit in stillness and listen
for the soft music

CRISIS OF FAITH

After Sunday service, in the basement of the church, over day-old Bear Claw and lukewarm coffee in a Styrofoam cup, a shrouded figure sidles up wearing a slouch hat with a black patch over one eye and slips me God's private number with a wink, but when I call from home all I get is an answering machine.

I gathered up my life edits from the cutting room floor and spliced them into an accelerating montage which was banned by the Elders next Sunday as too worldly and profane.

I quit going to church, turned off the lights and quite answering the door and, after a time, rumor had it the Reverend was drinking to excess and on occasion beat his wife when seized by the Holy Spirit.

I know my time is coming. The vacant smile of the newly resurrected creeps onto my face more every day. Whenever the kindred light of congregational amnesia breaks down the darkness in my den, I stop my ears and close my eyes as in myth sirens are often mistaken for angels.

I pinch my cheeks to bring out a blush, slap the stiffness from my legs as if to stumble half-conscious through the last round of a championship fight, hoping to win on points.

My point here is that the spirit rises as the flesh fails.

The sunburnt apple highest in the branches ripens too early. The apple in the shade remains stunted. The apples on the ground ferment.

I've found it most fruitful to be somewhere in-between—the liminal man in a grey world, embracing the uncertainty principle as proof enough.

Each time I consider giving up singing solo to take my place in the choir, I dream of a clatch of body snatchers with family Bibles standing in a circle around my bed coaxing Jacob in me to come out and climb his ladder.

An echo of doubt sounds the dark interior, a cynical habit of looking deeper elevates reason over faith, and I find myself wondering why I should sing the praises of a God that sponsors war and destroys the innocent along with the guilty, while those who survive believe selfishness, small-mindedness, and meanness must be condoned as virtues.

What if becoming more spiritual means becoming more unbalanced?

What if letting go of pleasure to avoid pain means letting go of the very instrument we need to know God in the first place?

The chemistry of loss is weakening my immunity to group therapy. I might end up just another worker bee in the fields of salvation losing his way back to the hive, my pockets full of pollen never to be made into honey, never to be savored on the tongue of anyone conscious enough to know sweet from sour.

They could come any day now to drag me off kicking and screaming down to the river's edge at twilight, to dip me into reflections of the moon, knowing full well I never learned to swim in that light.

When they pull me out of those depths sputtering like Ahab lashed to the back of Moby Dick, this beautiful, unearthly voice is singing to me. And I want to reach up and pull down this Angel of Mercy, wrapped in nimbus robes, her porcelain smooth face without visible cracks, and kiss her perfect lips. But the light is somehow wrong—warped or distorted as it passes through some dense medium.

The mask is ripped away and I am face to deformed face with the Phantom of the Opera.

I am running down a dark alley past homeless people living in cardboard boxes and, behind me, I hear the snapping of family Bibles, snapping open and shut, open and shut, like the jaws of a velociraptor, yellow lizard eyes tracking my thermal dodge and weave.

And all because some soul eater misinterpreted the only book he's ever read and totally missed the hidden story about finding God in man.

KOANS FOR PHYSICS MAJORS

Black holes have no depth
*

Some stars are not where they appear
*

Effects can precede their causes
*

The cat in the box is killed by curiosity
*

The human spirit is non-local, both particle and wave,
and can't be reduced to any one State
*

If looking up is looking back in an inflationary multiverse
then getting older is to become more isolated
and the closer you are to the end
the less you would recognize it
*

Dark Energy that cannot be seen yet has been measured
makes up seventy-percent of the universe
*

Seventy percent of the universe cannot be seen
but can still be Imagined
*

The Mystery cannot be created or destroyed;
it can only change its Mind.

RETIREMENT PARTY
PLAYA INSTITUTE, SUMMER LAKE, MARCH 25, 2012

I come to a clearing below the rimrock
where the wind makes waves in wild rye

A Mountain Bluebird hovers over the bowing grass
follows me down from juniper to willow to rose

Such blue cheer in a color-blind world is a miracle
a miracle to behold where a stiff Souther whips alkali

clouds a thousand feet into the air and the robust harrier
makes no headway along the pluvial plain

My boots accrue sodden earth as I trudge
down to water's edge while all the way

this little piece of sky chits and cheers
from shadows inside a thicket of wild rose

showing off on the rusted back of a disc harrow
presenting himself from the branches of still bare trees

Walking home I cruise along the highway and brace
for the bluster I hear gathering from behind

A semi truck blows by, never slowing down
nearly pulling me into its slipstream

I pass through the open gate into the yard
which sits comfortably off the road far enough

to resolve the Tristan chords of modernity into
a delicate balance between nature and appropriate technology

The bluebird no longer follows me
I consider changing my route next time

so I can maybe hold onto that giddy fellow
a little while longer

I open the back door where inside my work remains unfinished
where I talk to the world through screens and dials

pushing buttons, searching for the right key, the right color mix
turning machines on and off and living somewhere in-between

The fire by now is nearly exhausted, cold draft
augers through every unsealed crack in the walls

From the direction of the woodpile
I hear a *chit, chit, chit*, and discover the sky

is falling, one bluebird at a time until
the whole yard is azure standard bluebird

an internal combustion of lapis lazuli
an unsettled flutter declaring *we're here, we're here*

On the threshold I hesitate, feeling the tug
as balance shifts from living to thinking about living

from bluebirds to writing about bluebirds
from sensation to reverie

Fragments of blue sky blown to pieces
by gunmetal clouds plowing like battleships

through rippling reflections in a shallow lake
descend like fallout, calling me

from where I hover over the threshold
Chit, chit, chit, we're here, we're here

Today I was lucky enough to receive bluebirds
and pass them on to you

Tomorrow...?

FIRST EDITION

Mine alone
this book
Slipcover scuffed and torn
binding coming loose
spine jammed
edges tattered
margins violated
by momentary eurekas
forgotten once the page is turned
Still I cannot guess
its ending

Photo by Sue Memmott

About the Author

With *Lost Tranmissions*, **David Memmott** has published six books of poetry, a novel and a story collection. His poem, "Where the Yellow Brick Road Turns West," was a finalist for the 2010 Spur Award from Western Writers of America. *The Larger Earth: Descending Notes of a Grounded Astronaut* was selected as one of 150 best poetry books for 150 years of Oregon statehood by *Poetry Northwest* and Oregon State Library. He is a Fishtrap Fellow, a recent Playa resident and recipient of three Fellowships for Publishing from Literary Arts, Inc., for his work as editor and publisher of Wordcraft of Oregon, LLC (www.wordcraftoforegon. com). His new novel, *Canned Tuna*, is looking for an audience. He is also managing editor of *Phantom Drift: A Journal of New Fabulism*. He lives in La Grande, Oregon, with his wife, Sue, and two yellow labs.

SERVING HOUSE BOOKS

For information on other
titles, please visit our website
at:
www.servinghousebooks.com

www.ingramcontent.com/pod-product-compliance
Lightning Source LLC
Chambersburg PA
CBHW051843040426
42447CB00006B/667